For Debora

As long as the stars

feed on the fields of heaven

and the clouds move over the mountain valleys

shall your name be remembered.

—Virgil

Grateful acknowledgement is extended to the following publications in which these poems originally appeared:

Connecticut Review: "The Man with the Tuba"

The Evansville Review: "The Old Alley" and "A Scansion of Petrarchan Larks"

Los Angeles Times: "When the River Rises"

The Mochila Review: "To the Earth, Sea, and Sky"

New Letters: "The Mortar and the Pestle"

North Stone Review: "Leda on Lake Mälaren"

Ontario Review: "Hitchhiking to the Arctic," "The Aleutian Forest," "*Coeurage,* 'The Birth of the Heart,' " "Bowing Trees"

Poetry: "If for Each of Us"

Poet Lore: "Gibraltar and the Winged Moon"

Prairie Schooner: "The Treaty at Iwuy"

Rattalpallax: "Sometimes" and "The Bunker at the Vienna Augarten"

Rattle: "The Tower Window at Kosik," "Three Couples at a Trieste Stazione," and "Richmond Hill"

Transformation: "Knowing Warmth of Cloth," "Walking the Equator," and "Moving Everest"

U.S.1 Worksheets: "The Fate of the Universe"

Wilshire Review: "Our Lady of Brick Alley"

World Literature Today: "Wind on the Plains" and "After Too Long a Solitude"

Contents

If for Each of Us / 3

I
A Measure of Solitude

The Aleutian Forest / 7

Hitchhiking to the Arctic / 9

Harbin / 11

Moving Everest / 13

Wind on the Plains / 15

Walking the Equator / 16

Gibraltar and the Winged Moon / 18

Redwood / 20

Knowing Warmth of Cloth / 22

After Too Long a Solitude / 24

II

Mapping a Road

Bowing Trees / 29

Richmond Hill / 31

The Old Alley / 34

The Treaty at Iwuy / 35

The Midnight Strip at Faustos Beer Cafe / 37

The Bunker at the Vienna Augarten / 39

Leda on Lake Mälaren / 41

Three Couples at a Trieste Stazione / 43

A Scansion of Petrarchan Larks / 45

The Tower Windows at Kosik / 47

When the River Rises / 49

Reflections / 51

III

Crossing a Boundary

Heliopause / 55

Coeurage, "The Birth of the Heart" / 57

The Witch of Wookey / 59

The Mortar and the Pestle / 61

Our Lady of Brick Alley / 63

The Fate of the Universe / 65

The Man with the Tuba / 67

The Value of a Penny / 69

To the Earth, Sea, and Sky / 72

Finally There Is August / 74

Sometimes / 76

We should consider every day lost
in which we do not dance at least once.

Friedrich Nietzsche

I howl at the moon
with all my heart
and put the blame on the dogs.

Rainer Maria Rilke

If for Each of Us

a rope could swing us
long and light across a widening trough
of all that fails us in our lives,
I would want to land upon the Isle of Echo,
lush with repetition, green with being
original in birth and twice the twin
a wave might dance along the skerry.
I would want a canyon tall for hawks to carry
long the deep tattoo of voices on the air.
I would want an ear to hear
what words to read again to memory,
what verse to carol, thoughts to root
before the sparrow's flight the mind has taken
comes to rest on truth. I would want
to hear a vowel repeat in consonance
with alliteration's frothy throat.
And should the landing fail its footing,
I would want to know what inspiration
in shorter flight one syllable might repeat

as in the swash the flat-stone makes
to skip across the light in water
or the voice a wind gives to birch and linden.
I would want the distance to all understanding
to narrow just enough to fail at failure.
I would want a melody of chances
to learn to love again what first I dreamed,
free as wonder, soft as touch,
and of all things simple
to care again for them as much.

I

A Measure of Solitude

You have a great distance of trust to cross

The Aleutian Forest

It fails to grasp the predicament,
to be named a forest—a lone spruce,
digging into the rock's rigging
for nourishment in snow,
when all around it, stones are rootless,
and scurfs of ice tumble through flight.
It shares no iris fields to walk about,
no shade, no arbor's neighboring bark.
The ice, now gutted where the trunk
has hunkered down to seed its cones,
shods the whiskered stiles,
a grand ensemble for a bland horizon.
High above the thorny wreath
no terns assemble, no wind has crossed,
no echo of a fallen branch
has caused the cliffs to shudder.
No storm has passed. A fence leans near
to give the silhouette its silence,
to square it into comfort, a society of one.

How should it behave for generations
to live the life of boundaries
in the company of none?
How for recreation, should the sealskin
for its part, wet like peat,
surround and play inspired ground?
And should a feather fail to fall
from the egret's wing, what will give it song?

Hitchhiking to the Arctic

Any floe will do, but give it a name,
the Pater Noster, for a start, or the Isle of Latitudes
drifting north of Iceland out of Hudson Bay
in seas as mixed as the Bering Strait.

Choose the ice that's narrowed at each end,
the melting equal in duration, your little nation's future
dependent on the center clearing
any final reef the change of wind might make.

And deny all possibility that you're drifting
sunless and alone, that you're deranged, confused
by the solo berm on the map you yourself have sewn.
And deny, above all else, the albatross

whose wings you've sheared as windshields to the eyes.
You have a great distance of trust to cross,
so little of it bearing on a compass or a star.
You have only the dream of being lost a certainty,

that in the silence of the miles there will come
a conversation only you will hear. In that vast indifference
of the ice that drops its continents an inch each year,
you will survive on solitude each day or night

when even the moon your eyes betray
grows darker as you grow, and all around you
dance the petals of a sun burning in the cold blue of snow.
The light that draws you nearer is farther than you know.

Harbin

At Sun Island Park in the Chinese city
they carve out of ice each year,
the bridge they've whittled
lights its beams on panes of candled lanterns.
Beside the miniature Great Wall,
at forty below, cubed like dice,
a sculpted ship is land-bound into permanence,
its rudder arctic stiff. To its side
a mare, cut and tamed in stride,
kicks high within a block of glacial sun.
We await what image, dozing through winter,
will engrave its spirit in the river,
what grazing gull will call the spring to arrive.
The ice won't have it. The sun still sets at noon.
The Harbingers have too little
of nothing to grow. They would seed
more fire in the neon's slow melting

of a mural's night tern
if the sun could breed.
The ice won't have it. Nothing
will announce its departure from the snow.

Moving Everest

I think sometimes the earth
        moves quietly beneath me.
            I feel its skin shudder
        through the alchemy of wind,
as when the sun squints,
        amazing itself
            with embattled brilliance,
        Everest quivers
into an avalanche of clouds,
        and the ice melts
            into rivulets of light.
        In time rain, and all
of nature, is haloed at high ground.
        A rock blossoms
            out of mud, and shade
        out of the groves
of peach flowers.

Across the dark
                    obsidian fields
          trees flow greening
into a racing herd of colors
          among the foothills
                    of deodar. At dusk
          with the wet rag
of the moon
          wiping my windshield,
                    I see the high fallow buck
          sprinting a doe
into the hollow.
          All lovers find their way
                    into such affection
          through the trust of another.
Some mind it by solitude,
                    some by the measure
of a mountain,
          moving.

Wind on the Plains

I could watch for days the littering wind gives in to,
as in a train, always to sit alone facing the field
or the boortree as it slaps the sleet toward you
on the lamp-lit pane, and with what skill
to leave the distance passing like a gandy
dancing out of view, while a burdock, taller in its tow
quibbles past, the eyes a mirror withstanding
all that rain can do. It's not as though
the swift train passing leaves you standing still,
nor is it likely the coot that snows in feathers
will out-wing the smoke's long rail.
As long as I am moving forward, I would rather
see the field renewed, a squint of future bursting through,
a scud of sunlight, racing through the drumming drift of snow.

Walking the Equator

Some days if you squint lightly,
you will see the wet air of light a gull imagines,
the red cowries and docken leaves beneath,
the valerian that bleeds into soft fields of lavender,
kittiwakes that stripe the spines of ferns,
and skimmers with miles of perch to gather.
Shade each lash and brow
for just this moment,
and watch the sun pink its way through dusk
to build its own horizon, a strand of silk
above the sparse sprinkling of flamingos,
how the gorse will breed beyond its green
and balsa leaves repeat their minted amber.
And if at dawn you dream
the sky in rain, a sable cloth for dining,
the sun will walk the table blue until the dish is clean,
and every ladle of ocean the daylight sculls
will spoon up currents in infinite duendes of yellow
to wash the evening off.

Imagine all of this in darkness.
There will flow beneath the wake of trees a honeyed water
whose gold creased waves the stars will ride.
There will drift into lostness, a sun beyond the peak
whose moon, by reflection, will whiten all your nights.
With all things seemingly as one, imagine how solitary
in their disparate halves,

                    the hemispheres divide.

Gibraltar and the Winged Moon

In a field of aspen
on the Catalan coast,
while we dance the Sardana
in scuts of rue and chanterelle,
you ask why souls are lost.
You lift an eyebrow, think
a thought for hours
as if the question said
were skimming the corners of the sun
eternally. In your manner
of paradox you sleep
molding a swallow. Later
as we drive the coast of Andalusia
in no particular silence, your hands
fly out, releasing wings
so delicate and distant
the dark behind the sun begins to vanish.

An answer follows.
In time five winged moons
light the other half of earth;
an aureole of stars gilds Gibraltar.

Redwood

One might not see the point to it,
a redwood rising trunk to shaft,
why in sleep each night I hug the bark,
my feet stanced firmly in the roots,
and shouldering the lowest branch,
raise my eyes into the boughs
        and dance in silence
with the tree I will never marry.
And the tree kisses back knowing I am able,
how in a world of sun and swallows
the confusion is easy, to think the touch
of dying limbs skittling down
through raw wind to blackthorn grass
is the rush of hands reaching out
        to consummate the embrace
of a mind bereaved by solitude,
and knotted at the kneeling knee,

imagining what beyond the sky
the tree has known to make it reach,
perhaps a nesting moon or merle,
perhaps a generation's grief.

Knowing Warmth of Cloth

We were five in the bed, my brothers
shivering bones through all-day rain.
Outside, the winds had dammed up
mist in fields of glass on the front porch window,
and the sky lived high and wide, golding
well above the lightning's lambent seizure.
Where all night the spray's eternal voice
had tossed its notes beneath the awning's cape
in skids along the marble tiles and banister,
I'd shake the bed free of blankets,
dance the wool with body talk through blinding
threads of light, thunder-deaf. And breathing in
the jasmine scent, I'd swing
the back porch glider into torrents, legs kicking off
the harrowed hands of hail reaching in
to pull me further out into the world's indifference
and into darkness. I'd taunt the fireflies
whose little moons had romanced light into my mind

and pull the blankets level to the chin, knowing
warmth of cloth, the familiar wholeness of being
alone with my fears, and dry in my youthful gliding,
I'd close my eyes to the wind-sweep of my cold war years.

After Too Long A Solitude

I usually wake and walk about the city,
to free my breath, and with a word
brush the feathers of the tongue, softly,
through a whisper, to nudge the silence forward.
I wade in lugs of seaweed, always along the pier pilings
to be a circling wind to the dimpled waters
or a shout one judders like a pebbled can
to shape a timid voice to laughter.
At noon I load the morning's memory
with sounds of osprey, their walk-talk
clear and sleek as glass glimmerings.
By nightfall when the sky dissolves
into the red twinings of an intimate light,
I dance my words to the lute of a warbling tanager
and watch the fall moon lilt
into myriads of thatched kindling.

If I could breathe all words into infinity,
I'd drink beyond the mind
all of space an original thought inhabits.
I'd spare no passion in believing that it sings.
I'd touch the sun as if it were new,
as if for the first time to name a thing,
the rust in fire, cloth in stone. I'd carve the wind
with parting lips to know the ivory in its sensations,
as if a kiss like a gesture, formed a thousand times,
were immigrant to a foreign skin.
And always and in every dance,
I would want to hear each note passing into song
as a beat rising to crescendo, timeless as an insight
or a moon in the shade of the sun,
in spiral spins of inspiration, arriving
at once with being gone.

II

Mapping a Road

I have followed bends until the journey's end surprises

Bowing Trees

It is best to come upon them, off-road,
in a grove, usually at sunfall, near a lake
with its gaggle of pullets circling the birch—
four saplings, perhaps in pairs and opposite,
and tend to their ground as if the space were an altar,

where you bow their heads of leaves in twine,
shouldered one to the other in huddled relief,
then toss the blanket over to remove the stars
and planets from plain view, and lying beneath,
safe as a canopy, breathe in the moon.

Not for the poppels lined in a row
with the golden beech tree or the blue succory
on the banks, a stone's throw from the mosquito nest,
nor for the spring squill climbing the cliffs
with scents of foxglove and wild angelica,

but for the blossom of light at dawn
when the sun is in resurrection forever
and the genuflecting shadows from the hills spread wide
as umbels, their clustered leaves, soft as eiderdown,
to shade the way back to the road again.

Richmond Hill

It is my habit to walk a hill until it levels out
or until it thinks it has seen enough of sloth
and the way I map one foot flat in front of the other,
each step shorter, wider than the first, a platypus of sorts,
whose rhythm like its waddle I have borrowed since birth.

It is my habit to walk a hill until the sky falls near
and one believes he's risen to the heavens
where the Queen's deer sprint past sprigs and crockets,
and nighthawks graze above the Orchard House with such ascension,
heaven knows what royal robes the moon must wear.

I might sooner run downhill to find my level
because the road that rises up to meet me has no will
and bends to unimpede me like a gifting uncle,
wise and wily but in matters of frailty, unskilled.

I might even learn to hug the hill when it pretends to slope
at every lurch beyond the Terrace bole and heather
as if it grieved for the mind descending, and pulls the eye
back toward some higher view the road intended,
as when my breath searches for a swig of air,

there rises in the valley a swill of smoke,
and racing, I rabble thirst until the eyes tumble
downridge to the Nightingale's Meadow
where the field edges past the bunchgrass into a cattle grove.

There between the sparrowfall and woodsmoke like a rime
that winds along the center of a verse, the river bends
as is its habit when followed by so many feet as harrowed as mine.
And while it's not my nature to steal my way into the low roads
and fox lands where the marsh pine hugs the bracken,

I have followed bends until the journey's end surprises
and like the hawk above the Gothic turrets on the Old Main rising
high into its lofty fields of sky, I have wandered the Thames
from Richmond Hill to Kensington for the order nature gives my mind
and of the shorter roads have sought the longer one to climb.

The Old Alley

It has found the nights in Paris
swaggering tiptoe up a stair,
a taste too rich for browsing, and prefers
the simple lit barometer of a match
igniting the wet silk of an Antibes moon
into trellised strips above a drainage grate
or a vine curling about the window irons.
In its day it might have lured Picasso
in a Spanish mood, or lounged like the Maya,
spine-still, in the haze
and greening laughter of the leaves
or the rose shade of a stain-glassed sill
rising high into cathedral vaults.
When it wakes, it likes to round its shoulders
into each sleeve of a garden wall,
groomed with moss and wild wisteria,
and leap into a conversation or a photograph
for the rest of a day or night or year.

The Treaty at Iwuy

All week along the coast I chased cicadas
the lanky radio beat had found inconsonant,
and having lost direction to the Brussels road
whose spire I had mapped the headlights toward,
I found a hedge stooped low enough to shoulder-height
that roof beams pitchforked up on rungs,
and moonlight splintered through in golden flakes
to glow where once a bomb had skidded down.
The steam had popped the engine's trundle. A barn
in disemboweled appendage warmed the devil moss,
and feet my sleeping bag had parceled out
now claimed with fire, equal lots of land.

All night the rain had sung in distant riddles
to the cratered earth beneath me, and where the fog's
low wind preludes the lark's ancestral anthem
a breathing dared my mind to wake.
Above the croft like a tremor in the pestering rime that stammers,
the host of morning knelt: not the prince of manors

marking limits as in distance a river flows or dwells,
nor the scrivener's finger sketching trespass with a quill,
but a bull
with language so refined it swallowed sound,
as if by mourning it survived the world's occupation;
a force of nature feeding off the land, the lord of future
drinking from the well, reclaiming lost ground.

The Midnight Strip at Faustos Beer Cafe

In Ciudad Juarez my host says,
here on our stage a woman will undress,
and lights moon down slowly

the way a boy's eyes drag the bar,
sleep-shy, one wink at a time,
adrift like tossed boats. Hags,

hawking rosaries and chicken limbs,
spit-shine shoes on the rail
for the dime fee. My host,

the fat man, pulls off his toupee
when the fat girl declines
to drop her g-string.

He means by this to show nakedness,
that bald heads like billowing breasts
are flattering and sensual.

She thinks she understands
and turns each cheek, pouting lips to kiss.
It is unlikely they will communicate

their fears in the dark. He will glide
gently from his stool to the street.
She will dance to the last hollow heart,

change her name on the marquee,
and moving on, reluctantly
tease the boy's eye to sleep.

The Bunker at the Vienna Augarten

It is only a garden wall, and still
no one suspects that on the *Flakturm*
where the ivy worms its griddled skin
inch by inch along the gloried stone,
a worry grows within the hull,
that years have passed in lurid auguries,
and no one's walked the turret's ledge
or poked his hand into each dented eye.
The sign suggests it is forbidden
now to trespass through the lawns
of waffled hedge and crewels of marguerites
or to climb to see the Danube pass
beneath these silent stairs. It would seem
a duty now to blast the concrete through,

to whittle out a passage, to get at

what survives within the core. One might pity

this wart on the knee of a city,

refusing to kneel, or ascend, were it not

for the pigeons dead within its belly,

swallowed whole at the promise of flight.

Leda on Lake Mälaren

On Viewing François Boucher's Leda and the Swan
at the National Museum, Stockholm

It is at this image, teaked and flurried,
this scene unlike the others, wall enough
to paint Creation on the Sistine vault;
here where shade has trellised space in light,
and wakes of the tilled pond's fury
rake the gold in everything, a gilding
so unlike another, it haunts the nature of birth
as a condition of wonder,
and where the sky's premonition is boldly rain,
autumn armies forth, in wistful rouge
embattlements, a dream, no more a passing
than a memory, but as permanent,
in whose worried frame, the universe now grows
a burden—a swan has raped, and the empire's sun
falls to Pericles through some Shakespearean fate.
It is to this image, late, near dusk,

corporeal and grand, like no other,
that the craven tourist burrs the camera
into the muscle of air and flexing tight
the lens of his eye,
                    snaps the shutter,
instant as the flash, and scatting past
Renoir to Klee, one to the other, intends to save
each shot for a later pleasure, unencumbered
by the timeless awe the present view inspires,
and who will, as seeing such a wall demands,
carry home on film, his memory
of imitation, twice imitated, having passed on
the original for some other in the universe to admire.

Three Couples at a Trieste Stazione

1.

The first, Venetian lovers, with trysting hands
like birch branching through the window,
do not talk or breathe, but leafing her tongue
in words too thick for seeing, the girl
still wears her thought's perfume in smoke
a soldier dances into, backward, eyes saluting.

2.

The second, boarding baggage, knows the terror
that follows once the straps are hung
on shoulders or on rungs above the cabin sink.
He has packed the year's mementos greed has won,
his *nona* sliding *liras* into hands her eyes will bless
in thought each night against her cheek.

3.

The third will not survive the train's departure,
the kiss so passionately endured it quickens
as though in touch, their souls ignite in water
as in fire. They have passed what aging each denies,
and the body ruins their Tuscan masks disguise

will splinter into bones like timber, one onto the other.

A Scansion of Petrarchan Larks

It's a fact that brain cells of a songbird regenerate in April
when the ice stems pool for spring, and sunlight,
branching roots, clings to the kite
of a starling's wing growing violently still.
   And I believe that South is where the whimbrels go
   to free the dumb notes in their throats,
where yard larks in hawthorns croon to the deaf
as if to empty silence from their craws,
as if the first fall of rains in their beading vocals
might harmonize, silent as a finger signing off.
   If at night the bitterns want to fly
   toward sudden bursts of light, give them sky
to study hope. Let flamingos wing-glide when it snows.
Let all streams repeat their motion's thought
when man's intelligence is lost or a symphony robbed.

I believe that songbirds whimper for what is owed

      to lost beginnings, a melody renewed,

         as if by autumn they need no Southern flight to do.

It's a fact. I have listened to their notes, ubiquitous with dance,

inspire the mind, indifferent, to what nature has planned.

The Tower Windows at Kosik

for Ivan and Dasha Havel

From its eastern mooring, I watch a blue cloud
swing its loitering feet, and night's tall moon
leans on chimney stacks of nettled roofs.
Now a donkey clicks its hooves to a wooden beat.

On still another's night horizon, poplars sit,
just barely seen. I watch them plant thin arms
in hobo weeds as if to seed the southern pasture
with a pond for fish to glow in, gold before a fire pit.

And through the north pane's glare, the eye delights
in apples as in leaves, and dusk delays
to keep my daydreams green and growing free
as apricots in stacks of wood or gingko trees.

But in the west, reflections stow their thoughts
in glass so clear it mirrors the room in books
and all each seeks as worlds within me. Listen,
now departs my lost soul's journey into genius.

When the River Rises

for Prague underwater

When the river rises, a quail will lose its way
to diminution. The Kampa cove
creates a creek, trees are bushes, and islands
cupolas on which to gauze a wing.

When the river rises, the Charles Bridge
bellies down on legs, the stubbled arch
falls lame, and littered logs drift round
the carp and barges. A roof and crow

will sink in tow like pods to stems
when the river rises. And where St. Vitus spires
in their mist are gliding, clouds no longer
fix their tails to the slaked Vltava.

The shore is trebled into banks.
Reflections wade, a sea is made
in solemn visits. Swans above the seine
can barely stand the current's slubbing,

once the scuttle sinks to where the rocks
have muscled up a dam. In Prague
cobbles in the loam are freed of rain's translation.
Earth will make its way to shore again.

Reflections

When I lift my eyes I see
light above the shoulders of the sky,
a million suns, all in ascension,
and realize I have never seen the sun,
not one, in such proportion.

When I bow my head
to the mirror of the river, cupping the moon,
a million moons, all in suggestion,
I know that I have never seen the moon,
not one, in such illumination.

And when I close my eyes
and hear beneath the ice a new stream flowing,
a million rivulets, each a day's creation,
I realize I had never given thought
to the moon or sun or all infinity
until the earth had sung its song to me.

III

Crossing a Boundary

Your imagination . . . will leave you . . .
as divisible as light
in space, to spin with no boundaries at all.

Heliopause

*". . . the boundary at the sun that separates
the solar wind from interstellar space."*
—NASA Jet Propulsion Laboratory

Imagine that the planet Jupiter collides
each day with worlds invisible to our lens,
that in spinning, and as often as it matters,
it is cleaning up debris, all the meteors
and asteroids that laundry can gather;

that the earth, a deadened rock,
globed and wet for easy travel,
had once exploded past this celestial guard
to earn a space in the mapping's constellations.
Remember, there is in stone nothing
that hurls out a star. Imagine then in spite

of all we've heard or learned to give us order,
if, at the boundary of the sun, the winds of gravity
that bounce detritus toward the outer core's domain
would pause, for a millimeter of a motion,
how infinitely depressed by angst we would become.

Debris like astonishing thoughts would crash
in streams upon us, and wisdom as we know it
would dream the universe as one with night again.
Imagine that this will happen one day
when you wish the sun to rise earlier than dawn
and, failing gravity, your body falls
                          by the hollow drift
of your weightless heart. And your imagination,
as invisible and consuming as the universe,
it makes no matter what the matter, will leave you
when you least expect it, as divisible as light
in space, to spin with no boundaries at all.

Coeurage, "The Birth of the Heart"

Perhaps the skull was formed, the casing first
chipped from marble quarries near Alsace
where the red mud kilns to clay and skews of slate
seed odd signatures, thin as veins on a face.

The shoulder blades were carved more simply,
stony scythes honed to a razor cage
from which the arms were strung,
thin fiddle bows with little air to play.

Bones were added to distinguish legs,
that between two larger, a third, much shorter, hung
in desperation of a brain to gauge what reason
there was to love. Here no intellect was found.

The ribs were added as a packing crate,
cushions for the lungs, slivers of a lark's bone,
in whose incarceration breath was silenced,
hurled into flight by a lie shifting weight.

The heart was last to seed, a white rose rubbing up
against the bloodroot of the mind's red leaf,
and breeding the courage to imagine, the rarest found,
became in passion more often lost, most often blind.

The Witch of Wookey

I need no trolls or wraiths
>with whom to howl, no dog
>>to know just where to follow.
No moon, no skirt a flag
>>to hang above the doorway's mast.
>There's no point in looking
to find what's gone, what's past.
>She was the Witch of Wookey.
>>A laugh was dancing
on the wall of her soul.

She was a thief,
>whose laughter I renounce
>>and blaspheme to a priest,
as if to play the god
>>I could steal omniscience
>to change the story's clothes,
to keep her lie of romance,
>like imagination, free.

Each night in sleep,

        she worms her breathing through my ear.

            I get a little humid

then a little wet. She does not know

            the nomenclature of her gift,

      only that I die

a little with each breath.

And vowed to be alone,

        a sad and neutered hound,

           I howl at the moon,

to give her lie my dreaming.

            The soul I hope to save

      is now my own.

There is no point in looking.

      She was the Witch of Wookey.

           I howl to get the dog a bone.

The Mortar and the Pestle

One first thinks to keep the fingers clean
of substance, any matter soiled out of habit
or in passion. The mortar is a whore.
Now place the soul within, unscented,
sinner-cleansed and round in shapes
the eye won't fail to fashion. Nothing
so divides the invisible in matter
as the pestle in the hands of a lover,
not the driven thread through the crewel of silk,
not the knifing conscience, nor the pounding
stillness within the whole called center.
Nothing knows the absence of eternity
more than a soul the lover grinds
within the mortar's belly. Not this, not that.
Not the suddenness of now or nearly then.
Give the whore a dose of guilt
to breathe out a soul the world will smother.

Give a lover a soul, a space, or any hole to fill,
the end of the world will cease to matter.
In every act of love there is aggression
when you lose your soul to another.

Our Lady of Brick Alley

for James Wright

Each night as the mind knelt down
to see the slow parade of thighs
along the red-light shore of her window,
a pillow breathed a gladness in my loins.
Cats would root their teeth
in a hiss that showered moths for hours.
She had told me once to wink an eye,
that sinning girls are mortally forgiven.
For a dollar more I could wade
the shallows of her boy-shy eyes
to see my soul in full dimension
or dress the air in silks of sheer delirium.
She would never curse the river
I had crossed to wash my hands
of breasts she poured down infinitely
into choreographies of a lush language.

I would have begged for more
of a little light rain in the sky of her thighs.
She had taught me how, for all my sins,
to join so little for so much
at the drop of an eye.

The Fate of the Universe

We might have seemed a riddle,
borrowed from a book, characters drawn
rich in rimes, scurrilous, lazied by the stars
in some perfection of thought neither could prolong.
The park had wanted most to be
the legend in the scene, a lesser lover lost,
or a nymph with scents of jasmine
and a train of swans that browsed
and nicked the Pond's lip for pleasure.
We had dreamed too much of dreaming
well beyond the Bandshell steps, to the Loch, perhaps,
or where the Bow bridge had crossed the Ramble
into the lamplight of ascending spires,

or because the author, while omniscient,
stirred much deeper in our minds
his art's transcendence, an ancient frieze
of bodies balanced on the Boathouse stair,
where, unaware, each word

our tongues embraced had freed one breath.
In such a scene one would have the reader believe
no accident arrives by chance, no author leaves
to a god's uncertainty the fate of the universe
or to little more than strangers, the future
ordering of another.

The Man with the Tuba

Less than remarkable his swell of breath,
rushing through the bell and bore,
and hardly more the lips' small pursing
that he muzzles to the tuba's spout,
and no longer can he draw a wind
so deep it pouts in sighs along the brass
until the air is thinned into a bassoon's drawl,

when halfway up imagination's narrow stair
to where the lamplight's screen has shattered,
the tuba player stumbling, finds a woman
crawling deftly through the glass,
her paneless wire rims in hand,
and being neither deaf nor dumb,
is, nonetheless, sightless and alone.
                              And pleading
each to the other, one to grant a passage,
the other eyes to find the way,
they canter round in circles,

quick as cackling poppets pecking scraps,
how through the moon's supernal impasse,
each has lost direction, one his muse,
the other house and soul.

And reaching out to hold the other, the woman
begs to follow the tuba's bleating
to find the lost way home, and not to mind,
if with her cane they might arrange a union
to thump their notes into the night,
one with gasps of measured air, the other tapping
wood onto the stair each had never dared to climb.

The Value of a Penny

a.

You will find in the pulp of a pencil,
thin gray lead, of little value,
which by a punctured dent
>> can lead a word
to paper, light as nuance, dark as void.
You can find in the tube of a telescope,
a greater value, the seeds of constellations
>> in bottled space,
how by the intersection of a crossing spar,
an eye can measure what ahead is past,
perhaps a distant nebula
>> or the mystic universe
a bead of mercury occupies,
whose compass steers direction
to a star. The possibilities are vast.

b.

But give a pocket one raw penny
you've saved for laughter's awkward talk
when the finger's reach is longest
into sorrow, and even deeper
                in regret.
No lead can give it weight,
no axis of an eye can magnify it,
no mercury draw its head
                of Lincoln north.
And yet for what it's worth,
it will pay the highest value,
greater than the silver in a dime.
For the payment of a random thought,
when all your coins have fallen short,
                it will buy you time.

And while you're searching,

farther down your pocket's well,

you will score the meeting of a woman

who by the boldest intuition,

in order to arrive,

delays her entrance to the store

to give you time to settle up

your slug of copper life.

To the Earth, Sea, and Sky

for Tera, Mara, and Jameson

If while wading through the vale, you find in the hussock
long strands of wind tying grass around a violet
and knowing that it snows, you breathe it, lead it
out into the sun as if to teach it growth;

if in sleep you find the moon you dream won't still the sea
no matter how you pull its roots to shape
a roundness on the horizon, and smiling as you do,
you breathe into the tides their little pulls of gravity,

and if the planet's shift I promised hasn't tilted
on its stem, and stars the constellations free
to give the sky its dome's inspired limit
fail to light the firmament to grant you space,

then feed the water laughter, unfathom all you fear.
Keep the moon beneath you. Leap into its stream;
it will bathe you with the incandescence of reflections,

each of you in me. Climb it to the heavens
as you would the wind that braids a leaf.

You are my sun, my moon, my earth, my sea,
You are the universe in everything I need to be.
You are the ice pool still in winter, the paint in autumn leaves,
the crawl-shade in my summer, the birchbark clicking spring.
You are the incandescence of reflection, each of you in me.

Finally There Is August

As you walk the long hedge down the lane
in the raveled lay of dawn, and walking on
you see how high above the moonlit pines
a reed-tail flutters, back and forth,
to find its mate in married states
of pure elation, the stones look up,
the clouds lean down, and all you know
goes giddy round in night's imagination.
It is then you'll see how nothing new
that weds its face to winter gloom will matter,
not the door jammed stuck to icy bricks,
nor the aging eyes that blur to smoking candlewicks.
Nothing seems to matter, only moons you gather in
to store like spoons each May to feed your memory.
Then, and finally then, there is August,
when nightly you will breathe the scent
of jasmine buds in flight to pure ascendance.

And all that matters is the silence
you will share when sunlight frees all boundaries,
and all you see goes giddy free in your imagination,
and whisperings your minds will speak
will be like hands of stars embracing
all the words you've saved in life to say.

Sometimes

for Debora

Sometimes, and only if one dreams
as little of snow or of crows in branches,
and more of the woman who has come
softly to you, raising a brow toward a door
behind which a child crooks an arm
above a sleeping eye, the image will turn
to aureoles of dawn: gold, rose, vermilion,
each in their own language.

Sometimes, and only if it seems
so little of the night has scuttered
back into its cup, the word, *blue*,
like a runner out of breath,
will fade, unfurled, into a cheapjack strip
along a flag no longer striped,
and spread its satin palms, face up
into sunlight for only the sky of her smile.

And sometimes, and only in spring,
a dove from the river's soft vale of lilies
will fly as close to you as trust,
and a calm in the great reds of autumn
will, as often as you need, lie down
beside you, raising a brow you've known
above the eyes of the only woman
you will ever have a need to dream or touch.